THE HIDDEN LIFE of
Jesus

Deacon Norman Alexander

www.deaconnormanalexander.com

THE HIDDEN LIFE OF JESUS
Deacon Norman Alexander

Copyright 2013, Deacon Norman Alexander

No part of this book may be reproduced, stored in a retrieval system, or transmitted by any means, electronic, mechanical, photocopying, recording, or otherwise, without written permission from the author.

Editors: Dr. Marc D. Baldwin and Dr. Kevin of
http://edit911.com
Graphic Designer: Debbi Stocco, mybookdesigner.com

Scripture quotations are from THE NEW AMERICAN BIBLE

paperback-ISBN 13: 978-0-9912011-0-5
ebook-ISBN: 978-0-9912011-1-2

For information regarding permission, write to:
Permissions Department
5854 Sun Cove #1
Memphis, TN 38134

Or contact via website:
www.deaconnormanalexander.com

Table of Contents

Introduction 7

Chapter 1: Worship —Who, How, and Where 11

Chapter 2: The Woman as Savior 21

Chapter 3: Jesus, Savior of the World 35

Chapter 4: When Christians Make Christ Present 47

Endnotes 56

Acknowledgements 57

Dedication

These words I dedicate to my father and mother, Walter Alexander Jr. and Audrey Alexander. Your sacrifice for the sake of the family has allowed us to grow in the spirit of Christ, and we love you dearly for this.

Introduction

I FIRST HEARD OF BLESSED Charles de Foucauld while in the diaconate formation for the diocese of Memphis. As a class assignment, we were divided into groups of four and told to give a presentation on one of the saints or blessed. We had a list of names along with a book about each saint or blessed from which to choose. From this book, we were to learn about the person and do our presentation before the class. Our group waited until the last minute to choose a person for our presentation and all of the more popular saints such as St. Francis of Assisi, St. Teresa of Avila, and St. Augustine were already chosen. From the remaining three people, we chose Blessed Charles de Foucauld.

No one in our group had heard of Charles de Foucauld. After reading the book, I did not know what to think. I did not understand his life, philosophy, or spirituality. For instance, (1) *"Charles didn't feel called to imitate Jesus' public life of preaching, but he could see himself living in imitation of what* he imagined had been Jesus' life at Nazareth." Clearly, this is the hidden life of Jesus. My reasoning was if this part of Jesus' life was hidden, how could anyone know anything about it? My part of the presentation was the spirituality of the person we had chosen. It seemed the only thing left to do was to read the book for a second time. Maybe I had missed something.

Well, it turns out I had missed something very important, and now the essence of his life as a witness appeared to be unfolding before my eyes. Before finishing the book the second time I was blessed with this beautiful insight. Now, with a newfound excitement and enthusiasm, it was difficult to finish reading the book because I was anxious to write down what I received. Yet I was committed and knew that I would probably benefit from reading the complete book again. In the life of Blessed Charles de Foucauld, the hidden life of Jesus is obvious yet subtle. It is so in your face that it is hidden.

The hidden life of Jesus is his relationship with his mother the Blessed Virgin Mary. It became obvious to me why Charles said, (2) *"I love Our Lady of Perpetual Help."* Blessed Charles does not pretend to know anything about events during Jesus' hidden life. Rather he was living the experience of having Jesus within and making him present to others. I call this simple because we are all called to do exactly that, but never in my life had I seen it presented in this way.

Regardless of what spirituality a person choses to live by, understanding Blessed Charles' approach should enrich and enhance one's experiences as a Christian. I do not believe it would get in the way of anyone's discipline, because it is not a method or discipline, and there are no particular activities to add to a person's busy schedule. The only commitment would be to make an effort to understand the story. This is the most profound difference between the hidden life of Jesus and many other approaches to spirituality. Of course, there are the religious orders that follow a rule based on the spirituality of Blessed Charles de Foucauld, such as the Little Brothers of Jesus, the Jesus Caritas Fraternity of Priests, USA, and the Brothers of Charles de Foucauld Lay Fraternity.

Although I have spoken much so far about Blessed Charles de Foucauld, this book is not about him. It is about the hidden life of Jesus that is revealed in the life and writings of Blessed Charles. This has always been a part of the life of the clergy and religious, to make Jesus present in their preaching, teaching, and the sacraments, but the laity appear at times to not understand that we are all called to make Jesus present. Even without speaking a word, we should make Jesus present to others.

The story of Moses and his relationship with his mother, Pharaoh's daughter, his wife, and later Israel prefigured Jesus and Jesus' hidden life. From this point on, I will attempt to share these insights with you. Sometimes I will use simple charts to help demonstrate the cohesiveness of the story. Please do not be alarmed as you will not hear much else about Blessed Charles de Foucauld, other than how his life inspired me along with others to try to understand the hidden life of Jesus, and how I see it revealed in Blessed Charles' life. Anything more than this will have to be discovered by others reading about his life for themselves, as God may choose to give them different insights than those given to me. I hope you enjoy and find something valuable in reading this book. Thank you for considering it worthy of spending your precious time reading.

CHAPTER ONE

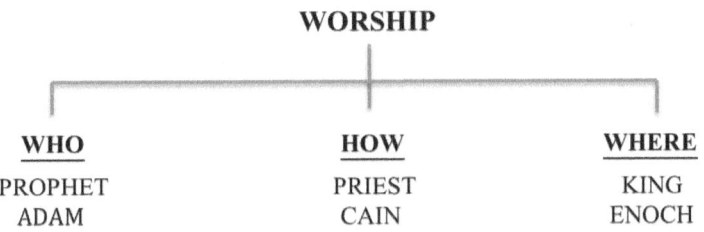

WORSHIP		
WHO	**HOW**	**WHERE**
PROPHET	PRIEST	KING
ADAM	CAIN	ENOCH

THERE HAVE BEEN MANY COMPARISONS made between Moses and Jesus. I am not interested in showing all of the comparisons that theologians have pointed out in the past, or even insights I have received. A particular theme has caught my attention that I will attempt to share. I would like to stress that it is one of many themes and it would be a mistake to consider it a summary or a complete story. Only God knows all things that make up the whole of truth. I believe God has blessed me to see this specific theme and I feel obliged to share it with others.

In the Baltimore Catechism, we are taught, (3) *"To gain the happiness of heaven we must know, love, and serve God in this world."* It is from this concept of truth the comparison can be made with the lineage of the firstborn Adam, Cain, and Enoch. Because of Adam and the original sin, when we come into this world we do not know God. When God revealed to Cain true worship and acceptable sacrifice, Cain rejected it. Thus, the descendants of Cain, who are cast out from God's presence, do not know how to worship the true God. Cain founded a city and named it after his firstborn, Enoch. This city represents that place where those who are cast out of paradise live and worship. In this context, to know, love, and serve God, is to know whom, how, and where to worship.

WHO TO WORSHIP—BECAUSE OF THE SIN OF ADAM WE DO NOT KNOW GOD

When Adam sinned, he listened to his wife and disobeyed God. We might ask why he did not listen to God and rather disobey his wife. In reality, the first offense was committed by the serpent, the woman committed the second offense, and the man committed the third offense. Our inheritance is from the man. God gave the man dominion over the earth and when he lost his dominion, we lost our inheritance. We have a new inheritance called the original sin.

The perfect order, which God ordained, has been disrupted. God is first because he is the creator. He is first before anything or anyone he created, whether visible or invisible.

Among his creatures in the corporeal world, man was first and woman was second. If the woman was having a conversation with an angel about the word of God, it was because she had rejected her husband's authority as the prophet. He was first in the visible world and the woman was his helper. She was a prophet because she was his helper, but once she refused to follow the man, who is the firstborn of God, she then became a false prophet.

The serpent—the leader of the fallen angels—betrayed God, because angels are messengers of God and should only reveal what God says. Their revelation should never supersede or contradict what God has spoken. Being superior in intellect and power, the angel was able to overpower the woman. Her husband should have been her protection from the deceitful angel. As the husband, he was a type of Christ, because Christ is the word of God made flesh. The first man foreshadowed our Savior in the sense that God gave him this order, (4) *"You are free to eat from any of the trees of the garden except the tree of knowledge of good and bad. From that tree you shall not eat; the moment you eat from it you are surely doomed to die."* He was the visible representation of the invisible word of God, which was within him. He was not the word of God made flesh as Jesus Christ is, but to the first woman he was first just as Christ is first to us, his bride.

If the Creator is first before his creation, and man is first in the visible world, then it is safe to say that our troubles, to a certain degree, began with the desire to be first. The angel who is a spiritual being desired to be first in the invisible world, and the woman desired to be first in the visible world.

The new order after sin entered the world is the serpent, the woman, and then the man. The serpent had gained dominion over humanity, and because man cannot see into the spiritual world, man does not realize that the devil is claiming to be the spirit of truth.

(5) *"The LORD God formed man out of the clay of the ground."* God is Father to the first man, and the earth is the image of a mother to the man. His father is the Spirit of Truth and his mother is the virgin earth. When Adam took the forbidden fruit from his wife Eve, she became his spiritual mother, because she gave him the way to eternal life, which she believed to be the truth. He was reborn of the woman and the serpent, the father of lies. This new order cannot work because the devil is a liar and a murderer and he cannot give life. Only the Creator can give life. What is more, the woman cannot lead the man because the body cannot lead the head.

HOW TO WORSHIP—BECAUSE OF CAIN WE MUST LEARN HOW TO WORSHIP GOD

Humanity has struggled in its quest to find the true God and the perfect order. Jesus Christ the only begotten Son of God revealed the Father to us, and restored the perfect order. He subjected himself to the will of the Father and restored the order of God, man and woman. The new woman—the church—follows her Savior Jesus Christ. She accepts being last, and does not try to become savior to Christ as the first woman Eve became savior to Adam. Although Jesus' body was the woman that tempted him in the garden, his agony did not lead him to sin. His response was, (6) *"Father, if you are willing, take this cup away from me; still, not my will, but yours be done."* He did not listen to the woman, those who tempted him to come down from the cross, because it was the will of the Father that he remained on the cross until the work of God was accomplished. The woman tempted Jesus to come down from the cross as Job's wife tempted Job to curse God and die. By his obedience to God and ignoring the woman, Jesus was able to reconcile us with the true God, and release us from the dominion of the devil. We have a new inheritance in the new man Jesus, the inheritance of eternal life in the kingdom of God.

    All of humanity came from the body of the first man, Adam, beginning with the first woman whom God built up from one of the man's ribs. All descendants of Adam come into the world through the woman. Thus, the seed that leaves the man's body comes through the woman and enters the world. The world we enter is under the dominion of the devil. Fortunately for us, God has a plan of salvation that allows humanity to return to paradise. We leave the world by entering the woman, the church. We enter the womb in baptism and return to the body of the man. We return to the body of the new man Jesus Christ. He is the second Adam and when we return to the body of Adam, we are back in paradise.

WHERE TO WORSHIP—WE RETURN TO DWELL AMONG THE SERVANTS OF GOD

This place of worship is for those who accept the worship that God has declared the acceptable sacrifice. Jesus and his sacrifice are acceptable to God. As we pray in the Divine Liturgy, (7) *"as once you were pleased to accept the gifts of your servant Abel the just."* If only Cain could have accepted that God favored Abel and his sacrifice, then Cain's sacrifice could have been offered along with the sacrifice of Abel. Instead of accepting Abel as first, Cain responded with the envy of the serpent and the woman. Perhaps he desired to be first spiritually because he was born first, just as the serpent desired to be first because he was created before Adam. First born of the flesh, Cain desired to be first as his mother did. Cain thus became a liar and a murderer like the devil. Cain inherited his disposition when he inherited original sin, but Cain committed the first actual sin. His descendants cannot inherit the sin of murder, but they are cast out from God's presence. This is the effect of the great apostasy: the children are born outside and cannot enter the temple of the true God to worship Him.

Jesus made it possible for us to reconcile with God and to return to the worship of paradise. On the cross, the thief on the right recognized his sin and accepted his place. He realized that he was not equal to Jesus and said, (8) *"Jesus, remember me when you enter your kingdom."* He replied to him, *"Amen, I say to you, today you will be with me in Paradise."*

The word *"remember"* highlights the essence that Jesus must enter his kingdom first, thus this man no longer desires to be first. Moreover, Jesus accomplished that for which his Father sent him. Paradise is now open to us again. We have a new High Priest, an Acceptable Sacrifice, a King who protects and conquers, and a Brother who leads us back to paradise.

Jesus is worthy of our praise and worship because he is God, and he has made himself known to us. John the beloved disciple explains that love is how we worship. The place we worship is the place that Jesus has made his dwelling. As when John and Andrew asked Jesus, (9) *"Rabbi, where are you staying?"* Jesus' response is, *"Come and you will see."* John witnessed Christ's crucifixion and resurrection. He took Our Blessed Mother into his home, in essence taking the Ark of the Covenant into his home. He is priest and servant of the one true God. Our place to worship is among the servants of God, because this is where God has made his dwelling. From Christ himself, the Word, the altar, the tabernacle, our worship, and our ministries flow.

Those who live in the city of Enoch may now return to paradise, but only if we accept the sacrifice of Jesus Christ. If we accept that Jesus is first and favored by God, we may offer our sacrifice from the earth. The bread and wine now becomes acceptable to God. The mystery of transubstantiation allows our sacrifices to be offered with the sacrifice of Christ. What can compare to the love of Christ who gave his life for those who did not love him, but instead had contempt for him? He gave his life for those who were willing to put him to death. The true worship is love. When we learn to love God and neighbor, we may return to paradise.

The following chart illustrates the hidden life of Moses. The six cycles summarize a horizontal view, which covers the span of Moses' life. The last three can also be placed directly beneath the first three as two vertical sets of threes. Moses' infancy is divided by three events, as in the life of Adam, Cain, and Enoch. From the time that Moses was adopted by Pharaoh's daughter, his life was divided by three events that reflect the life of Adam, Cain and Enoch. In Chapter Two, I will attempt to explain the meaning and theology behind this chart. It reveals cycles in history, and in my view offers compelling evidence that God is the Author of history.

THE HIDDEN LIFE OF MOSES; HE WAS NEVER SEPARATED FROM THE WOMAN, BUT LIVED IN A CYCLE OF CONCEPTION, GESTATION, AND BIRTH.

3 MIRACLES - This is the finger of God.
7 PLAGUES - Judgment on the gods of Egypt.

WORSHIP

WHO	HOW	WHERE
Prophet	Priest	King
Adam	Cain	Enoch

WORSHIP

WHO	HOW	WHERE
Prophet	Priest	King
Adam	Cain	Enoch

CONCEPTION	HIDDEN	RETURNED TO HIS MOTHER	ADOPTED BY PHARAOH'S DAUGHTER	MARRIED ZIPPORAH	CROSSED THE RED SEA
9 MONTHS	3 MONTHS	NURSED	40 YEARS	SPENT 40 YEARS TENDING FLOCK	SPENT 40 YEARS IN THE DESERT
BIRTH	EXPOSED	GIVEN TO PHARAOH'S DAUGHTER	LEFT EGYPT TO ESCAPE DEATH	GOD SENT HIM BACK TO EGYPT	ASCENDED MOUNTAIN TO GOD AND DIED

PHARAOH'S DAUGHTER SAVED HIM
Drew him out of the water.
SHE HELD ON TO HIM
Paid to have him nursed.

SHE SAVED HIM
Circumcized the boy and touched Moses with the foreskin.
SHE HELD ON TO HIM
You are a spouse of blood to me.

CHAPTER TWO

The Woman as Savior

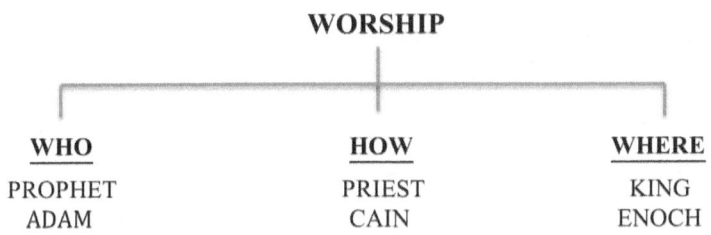

God gave to the first man dominion over the world. In addition, this first man is the temple in which all human beings come from, beginning with the woman, whom God formed from the man's rib. The man had dominion until the fall, when the man and woman sinned against God. When the woman believed the serpent to be the spirit of truth, she gave the forbidden fruit to her husband. She became savior to her husband. Although not really a savior, but moreso a stumbling block, and she retained this role until Jesus came to restore order. Her place as mother seems to signify that God allows her to retain this position even now in God's plan of salvation.

I would like to jump over to the story of Moses and his relationship with his mother, then Pharaoh's daughter and later his wife, and at last his relationship with Israel. This I hope will be a good illustration of how the woman continued her role as savior in the plan of salvation. In the fall of man, the woman was overpowered by the devil when he deceived her. Yet, God uses the woman to overpower the devil as he delivers humanity from the bondage of slavery to the devil.

Notice that Moses, like every one of us who inherits the original sin, came into the world with something of which to be ashamed. This is the sin that Adam was ashamed of, and the reason why he hid from God. In every pregnancy, the child is naked and hiding, and goes unnoticed until it becomes apparent that the mother is pregnant. The original sin inherited at conception blinds us, and we do not know God. We are capable of knowing God, but we must be reborn and reject Satan. Once we give ourselves over to God, it is possible to understand what the church teaches us about God.

The Egyptians, or at least the gods of Egypt, must have been aware of man's ability to know God, because the Egyptians ordered the midwives to kill every baby boy during delivery. God was going to save the Israelites from slavery in Egypt. He would send a savior to lead them out of Egypt. This savior would not be a woman, but a priest like Adam. God would show forth his power and give his word through this savior as with Adam before the fall.

In order for the Israelites to be born out of slavery in Egypt, they would have to be born out of paganism. They would become a people, a holy nation, and a royal priesthood.

To be born out of paganism is to be brought out of the culture of worshiping many false gods into a people who worship the one true living God, the God of Abraham, Isaac, and Jacob. This reveals that there was more to the slavery in Egypt than manual labor. The slavery was also to false gods.

Therefore, when Moses was born and the midwives did not put him to death, his mother knew that she had to hide him. She hid the child because he came into the world a fugitive in the manner that Cain was a fugitive. If anyone saw him, they would kill him, so she hid him, and in this way she was a savior to him. First, Moses was hidden in her womb for nine months, because the Egyptians did not know whether she was pregnant with a boy or a girl. She provided a sanctuary and safe place for her child. For nine months, he was nourished and cared for by his mother. At the end of nine months when she gave birth to a son, she knew that he would be judged, condemned, and put to death.

Adam also experienced this fear of being judged because he and his wife had given themselves over to a false god. Realizing that it was not possible to serve God and also the serpent, he feared being judged by God. When God called out to him, he responded, (10) *"I heard you in the garden; but I was afraid, because I was naked, so I hid myself."* Why? No one who is guilty of sin looks on the face of God and lives. Likewise, the Egyptians killed the baby boys because of the relationship this savior to be born had with the one true God. The false gods were judging the children at birth to prevent the people from being saved by the true God.

Everyone is free to serve God or not serve God, but no

one is free to leave the false gods without retaliation from these false gods. We can compare this to law-abiding citizens being free to remain law-abiding citizens or to choose criminal activity. Once a person has lost his freedom and is imprisoned, he is no longer free to choose a life of freedom outside of prison; he is forced to serve his prison term. God gave man freedom to choose, and, when man was cast out of paradise, we notice that God's judgment was merciful. God had a plan of salvation for the man and his descendants. Man may return to God if he chooses to do so, and God will accept him and assist him. It was not so with the gods of Egypt, their judgment was death, extreme suffering, and oppression in order to keep the Israelites enslaved. They imposed the judgment of death to anyone who attempted to break free and serve the true God.

During all of this time, Moses mother fulfilled her purpose as savior to her son by hiding his gender for nine months. She was also savior to her husband by preserving the offspring through whom he continues to live.

At the moment of birth, his gender was no longer concealed, so she had to hide him again. She hid him for three months, and we have the impression of her conceiving again. During the three months that the child was hidden, she nursed and cared for him. This was similar to the period of gestation that we see during nine months in the womb. She gave birth to him when she exposed him on the banks of the Nile. She placed him in a papyrus basket, which was daubed with bitumen and pitch. This part of the story reveals the same pattern of conception, gestation, and birth. The infant was floating in the basket along the banks of the Nile, just as Noah and his family were in the ark, during the flood. This was another time of judgment when Moses faced a life or death situation. He first faced life or death when he was born and later when his mother placed him in the basket among the reeds on the riverbank.

Then appeared on the scene a new savior, and it was the Pharaoh's daughter. She had pity on the Hebrew child, and had him drawn out of the water. Moses' sister was standing by waiting to see what would happen to the child, and she immediately came to Pharaoh's daughter and asked her, (11) *"Shall I go and call one of the Hebrew women to nurse the child for you?" "Yes do so," she answered. So the maiden went and called the child's own mother. Pharaoh's daughter said to her, "Take this child and nurse it for me, and I will repay you."* Now Pharaoh's daughter had become a new savior to Moses. She brought him out of the water in which he was exposed to death. But she also desired to hold on to him, and this is why she paid to have him nursed. Whoever nursed the child was doing it for hire and knew that the child belonged to the woman who was paying to have him nursed.

This was the second time that the infant Moses escaped death. The first time at birth, he escaped a judgment in contrast with the judgment Adam attempted to escape. The main difference being that Adam did not want to be judged by *God*, but Moses was in danger of being judged by *the false gods of Egypt*. Moses was not guilty of anything; he only inherited the sin from Adam. But, this second time when Moses escaped death, he was in the predicament of Cain. If anyone saw him, they would have killed him. After his mother hid him for three months, Pharaoh's daughter appeared as a savior to him.

This next time that Moses' mother took him in, if we are allowed to use our imagination further, he was conceived a third time. This however is only symbolic, and it means that his mother took him in again. She received him again into his own home, among his family, his relatives, and his people—the Israelites. He was now in a safe place, because Pharaoh's daughter had agreed to take him as her own child. The child Moses appeared to be in the womb again being nursed by his mother.

Now that Moses lived in the city of Goshen, he was in a safe place much like the city of Enoch. This was the city that Cain built and named it after his firstborn son. It was a city of refuge in which Cain could not live in because he was a murderer, yet his descendants could live there, because the sin of murder cannot be inherited. Corresponding to this, Moses was no longer a fugitive. He lived in the safety and refuge of the city. When this period ended, his mother exposed him again as though she was giving birth for a third time. And she gave him to Pharaoh's daughter. This brings to conclusion three periods of conception, gestation, and birth. This next section reveals a repeat of these patterns, although with very different circumstances.

Pharaoh's daughter adopted Moses and, as I stated earlier, the story began to repeat itself, because we again have the image of the child being conceived. He was brought into Pharaoh's household, which was probably as dark as it was in the womb of his mother. I say this because the gods of Egypt filled this household. As we know there is only one God, and he is the light. All false gods are of the kingdom of darkness.

So again, Moses entered a place of darkness just as Adam did when he listened to his wife and disobeyed God. There is a difference in that Adam subjected himself to the serpent, but his descendants are subjected to many serpents. The words of the serpent in which the first woman conceived were like the poisonous venom of a serpent, which brings suffering and eventual death if not cured. Moses, being a descendent of Adam, was in this household of false gods, which illustrates our predicament in a world of false gods.

When he was 40 years old, Moses was faced with a decision to serve the gods of Egypt or to turn to the God of his people, the God of Abraham, Isaac, and Jacob. As we know, Moses decided to look after the needs of his people, who were suffering cruel injustices. He killed the harsh Egyptian taskmaster who was abusing an Israelite. Moses judged the taskmaster, and by doing so he rejected the gods of Egypt, who were represented by Pharaoh's authority. Moses fled for his life and death passed over him, but death did not pass over the Egyptian taskmaster. Thus, Moses' exodus from Egypt foreshadowed the exodus of the Israelite people when God would save them 40 years later. Here again we see that the woman took Moses in, much like being conceived. Moses lived there for a period of about 40 years corresponding to 40 weeks in the womb, and then he was born out of this sanctuary. Again, he faced a judgment that could determine whether he lived or died. Moses escaped death just as Adam escaped death in Genesis 3 when God provided a plan of salvation for Adam and his wife Eve. There was no plan of salvation for the serpent. The serpent is cursed. Similarly, there was no plan of salvation for the cruel Egyptian taskmaster, he was punished with death.

Moses fled Egypt and ended up in the desert living with Jethro the priest of Midian and his family. He married Jethro's daughter Zipporah, and he spent 40 years tending his father-in-law's flock. We do not have much information about this period of his life, but at the end of 40 years, God appeared to Moses on Mount Sinai in the burning bush. And God told Moses that he was sending him back to Egypt to free the Israelites from slavery. This would end another 40-year period symbolic of a 40-week gestation in the womb when Moses left his father-in-law's household. This period that Moses spent was again like the life of Cain, a fugitive. If he went back to Egypt he would be killed, because he had killed the Egyptian taskmaster. Eventually, Moses would no longer have to live as a fugitive because it was evident that the Pharaoh had died, and there was a new Pharaoh.

An interesting part of this story is that God sent Moses back to Egypt, and along the way, (12) *the LORD came upon Moses and would have killed him. But Zipporah took a flint knife and cut off her son's foreskin and touching his person she said, "You are a spouse of blood to me."* Then God let Moses go. This event foreshadowed the blood of the innocent victim that protected those who were guilty. It foreshadowed the blood of the Passover lambs on the doors of the Israelite homes when death passed over their firstborn. But it also reveals that Moses' wife saved him from death. This continues the pattern where the woman was a savior to the man. Like Pharaoh's daughter, Moses' wife wanted to hold on to Moses, as she commented, *"You are a spouse of blood to me."* This sounds like a blood covenant, and Moses appears to have escaped death once again.

God sent Moses back to his home, among his people in the city of Goshen. When Pharaoh's daughter sent him back, he lived under her protection, because she intended to bring him back into her household to be of service to the gods of Egypt. Things were quite different when God sent Moses back. He was sent to free the Israelites from slavery to the Egyptians. This meant that Moses was now under the protection of the one who sent him, the Almighty God. It is obvious that he had always been under the protection of God and his whole purpose in life was to serve God. But I am merely drawing a parallel between Pharaoh's daughter who desired that Moses would serve the gods of Egypt, and God who sent Moses back among his people so that Moses could lead them back to serve the one true living God.

The pattern of the story now changes with the miracles that prove there is only one God. We first see the confrontation between God and the gods of Egypt, symbolized by Moses' staff that turned into a snake and the staffs of Pharaoh's magicians, which also turned into snakes. When Moses' snake ate all of their snakes it became obvious that Moses' God was more powerful than the gods of Egypt. After the third miracle, Pharaoh's magicians realized that (13) *"this is the finger of God."* Although it was Moses and Aaron who were performing the miracles, it was actually God who had come to judge the gods of Egypt. They could not turn the dust into gnats because only the Creator can bring forth life from the dust. Once God had established himself as the One they were dealing with, he inflicted the Egyptians with seven plagues. At the end of the seven plagues the Israelites were allowed to leave Egypt, thus they were set free from the bondage of slavery in Egypt. After the seven plagues that ended with the death of the firstborn of Egypt, God revealed that he came to pass judgment on the gods of Egypt.

One last time I would like to revisit the cycle of conception, gestation, and birth, and, at the time of birth, judgment. This time conception would happen when the Israelites crossed the Red Sea. They were baptized into Moses. Now we are able to see how God was restoring order. The savior is now a man and a priest. He is a prophet and a judge. Although Moses began to intervene as savior between the Israelites and the cruel Egyptian taskmaster, and between his future wife's family and the shepherds, his role was official and solidified once he was sent by God. The woman—Israel—has returned to the side of the man just as Eve was taken from the side of Adam. Now Israel was born as a people. It is the story of one man and one woman. The period of life spent in the desert was 40 years. So Moses had another period of 40 years, symbolic of 40 weeks in the womb. And after 40 years of shepherding the children of Israel, God called him up to the top of Mount Nebo to look at the Promised Land, which he would not enter. After he had a chance to gaze on the Promised Land he died and the Israelites saw him no more.

There were actually two groups in the desert with Moses. One group was living the experience of Cain. They were restless wanderers on the earth, all the days of their lives. If they tilled the soil, it would not give its yield, so each day God gave them manna to eat. These were the people who looked back to Egypt, and longed for the gods of Egypt in their hearts. Their story is like the story of Moses tending his father-in-law's flock in the desert for 40 years. The other group consists of those less than 20 years old when the census was taken. This group looked forward to entering the Promised Land. They crossed over the Jordan into the land of Canaan, which was more like the city of Enoch.

Note that the life of Moses always appears to be hidden within the woman. Whether it was his mother, Pharaoh's daughter, or his wife, his life was hidden until he was exposed at birth. He was always in danger of being killed when exposed. To summarize, first the midwives were told to kill the baby boys at birth. Then Pharaoh's attendants were told to throw all of the baby boys into the Nile River. Moses also faced death after 40 years in Pharaoh's household. Again, when on the way back to Egypt to free the Israelites, he faced death.

Was it safer for Moses to remain hidden? He would probably avoid being put to death by men and fallen angels, but the will of God would not have been accomplished. So this was not an option for Moses. He must have a hidden life, but it was extremely important that he was exposed at the moment of birth. This is one of the main reasons why, when looking at these illustrations, it is obvious that God has a plan of salvation; and Moses' life and his story foreshadowed the life and story of our Savior Jesus Christ.

The following chart is a schematic view of the hidden life of Jesus. Chapter Three explains the parallels between the hidden life of Moses and the hidden life of Jesus. The two charts are so similar that we can compare them vertically.

The Woman as Savior | 33

THE HIDDEN LIFE OF JESUS; HE WAS NEVER SEPARATED FROM THE WOMAN (HIS MOTHER), BUT LIVED IN A CYCLE OF CONCEPTION, GESTATION, AND BIRTH.

> 3 DAYS - This is the Son of God.
> 7 DEMONS - Cast out of Mary Magdalene.

WORSHIP

WHO	HOW	WHERE
Prophet Adam	Priest Cain	King Enoch

WORSHIP

WHO	HOW	WHERE
Prophet Adam	Priest Cain	King Enoch

CONCEPTION	HIDDEN	RETURNED WITH MOTHER AND FAMILY	ACCEPTED AS KING OF ISRAEL	ENTERED THE ABODE OF THE DEAD	APOSTLES RECEIVED THE HOLY SPIRIT
9 MONTHS	30 YEARS	STAYED A FEW DAYS	4 DAYS	40 HOURS	40 DAYS
BIRTH	EXPOSED	LEFT FOR JERUSALEM	CRUCIFIXION	RESURRECTION	ASCENSION

> JESUS IS THE SAVIOR
> Fill the jars...Draw some out.
> HIS DISCIPLES HELD ON TO HIM
> They began to believe in Him.

> MARY MAGDALENE TRIED TO SAVE HIM
> Tell me where... and I will take Him.
> SHE HELD ON TO HIM
> Woman do not hold on to me.

CHAPTER THREE

Jesus, Savior of the World

WORSHIP		
WHO	**HOW**	**WHERE**
PROPHET	PRIEST	KING
ADAM	CAIN	ENOCH

THE ISRAELITES DID NOT HAVE a king, because God was their savior. Moses was a savior in the sense that he was a judge, but God was truly their savior. When we begin to compare Moses' story with Jesus, there are many differences, which at times demonstrate a strong contrast, although we are making comparisons of similarities. The first and main difference is that Jesus is God and he is King. Jesus is the true Savior of the world, just as God was Savior to the Israelites. And he began his life among humanity when he was conceived in the womb of his mother, the Virgin Mary.

WHO TO WORSHIP

The incarnation, when compared with the story of Moses, reveals that a child has been conceived, but this child Jesus has nothing to be ashamed of, because he did not inherit the sin of Adam. Instead of inheriting a darkened intellect, as we do, Jesus enters the place of darkness as the light shining in the darkness. As written in the Gospel of John, (14) *the light shines in the darkness and the darkness, has not overcome it* During the Visitation when the sound of Mary's voice reached Elizabeth's ears, the Holy Spirit filled Elizabeth and the child in her womb. It is clearly a demonstration that Jesus came to free humanity from sin. The Spirit of God entered the waters and freed the child John the Baptist of original sin; a very stunning accomplishment, especially since Jesus himself, by the standards of today's world, was only a fetus a few days old.

Jesus came into the world without sin, and it was important that his Blessed Mother was also free of sin. This is difficult for some people to accept, but the new Adam and the new Eve had to begin life as the first Adam and Eve began life. They had to enter the world in original innocence and justice, in order for their decisions to have an effect on all of humanity. Both Jesus and his Blessed Mother needed to be free of sin, because through them God formed a new creation.

A slave cannot free another slave, and Jesus explains, (15) *"Amen, amen, I say to you, everyone who commits sin is a slave of sin. A slave does not remain in a household forever, but a son always remains. So if a son frees you, then you will truly be free."* If the Son of God frees you, then you are truly free. The Blessed Virgin Mary, once she accepted God's will, meaning the word of God, she had reversed what our first mother Eve did. Now it was up to Jesus to reverse what the first Adam did, in order to reconcile us with God.

Since our inheritance of original sin and death came from Adam and not Eve, our inheritance of the forgiveness of sin and eternal life comes from the new Adam and not from the new Eve. Our inheritance surely comes from Jesus, but the Blessed Virgin Mary is his helper. She is his helper as Eve was meant to be Adam's helper. So the new Adam and the new Eve are both without sin, and we can be reborn into their family and freed from our sins.

This is the freedom that the gods of Egypt were trying to prevent the Israelites from being born into. This is the freedom that the demons were trying to keep people they possessed from gaining. This is the freedom that Satan, the ruler of this world, is trying to prevent us from gaining. Although it seems that Jesus' battle is with humans that resist his mission, it is mainly a spiritual battle.

Jesus was judged the moment he was exposed. And those who judged him had condemned him to death, but God his Father had a plan to save him. Even before he was born, there was a threat to his life. Because of the census that Caesar had ordered, his mother would have to travel up to the time of her delivery. It is highly probable that if the census revealed that St. Joseph was the human father of the true King of the Jews in the lineage of David, then Jesus would have been exposed even before he was born. This circumstance was similar to the baby boys in Egypt when their gender was exposed during delivery. The journey to Jerusalem threatened the life of the child Jesus before his birth.

If Eve knew whom to worship by obeying the word given to Adam, her husband, and Israel knew their God by observing the law which God gave through Moses, then how much more can humanity know God through Jesus Christ, his only begotten Son? More glorious than Adam or Moses, Jesus is not only the Prophet but also the Word of God. To accept Jesus as Brother makes us sons of God. Jesus revealed the true God to us and reconciled us with God. The Magi, the shepherds, and later all of Israel were led to Jesus, because he is the image of the invisible God.

HOW TO WORSHIP

The child Jesus in the womb was the new Adam; he faced the possibility of death due to exposure. He and his mother survived the journey and the dilemma she faced of not being able to find a safe place to give birth to her child. After nine months, when Jesus was born, he, like Moses, was in danger of death. As soon as his mother gave birth to him, those in authority sought to put him to death. King Herod had all the baby boys two years old and under put to death. Herod was trying to kill the newborn King, not only because of a political threat to his throne, but there was something happening in the spiritual world that would free humanity from slavery. And the one who would save humanity is God, the same God that saved the Israelites from slavery in Egypt. Jesus is called King of the Jews because he offered salvation to his people first, but afterwards offered salvation to the rest of the world.

Just as Cain killed Abel, the rulers of the world desired to kill Jesus, who was not only the perfect sacrifice but also the high priest. He would later lead us to true worship and teach us how to worship.

Death, however, passed over Jesus, and his family fled to Egypt. This began the hidden life of Jesus. He had a hidden life of 30 years, compared to Moses' hidden life of three months. Jesus had a hidden life because if anyone saw him they would have killed him. Jesus had to leave Jerusalem, which is where the Temple was, the dwelling place for God's name. This is the burden that Cain expressed to God (16) *"My punishment is too great to bear. Since you have now banished me from the soil, and I must avoid your presence and become a restless wanderer on the earth, anyone may kill me at sight."*

We know little about the hidden life of Jesus except the story of him being lost for three days. We know that the holy family went to Jerusalem each year for the feast of Passover. At 12 years old, Jesus appeared ready to assume his responsibilities as the Son of God, and he expressed that he had to be in his Father's house. It was not time for him to begin his public ministry, so he went home with his parents, and was obedient to them. It appears they would not allow him to be born prematurely. He had to remain with his mother for 30 years, until she believed it was time to expose him. And when she did, it was like giving birth to him again.

At the wedding feast at Cana, Mary exposed Jesus. She interceded for the people and told Jesus, (17) *"They have no wine."* Then she said to the servers, *"Do whatever he tells you."* So it was a two-way intercession. Jesus had them fill the jars with water, and the six stone jars were filled to the brim. Then he told the attendant, *"Draw some out now and take it to the headwaiter."* Moses' mother exposed Moses in the Nile River. Similarly, Jesus mother exposed Jesus, at the wedding feast at Cana. Moses was drawn out of the water. Since the Old Covenant was in the flesh, Moses himself was drawn out of the water, because he is the lawgiver. Jesus instructed the attendant to draw some water out. Jesus was to give the Holy Spirit, establishing the internal New Covenant. At this time Jesus disciples began to believe in him, which meant they desired to hold onto him.

WHERE TO WORSHIP

Jesus returned home with his mother, his brothers, and his disciples just as Moses returned to his mother and family in the land of Goshen when Pharaoh's daughter paid to have him nursed. Jesus stayed with his family and disciples a few days before he went to Jerusalem.

It was most desirable to worship in Jerusalem in the

temple of God. Yet, because of sin, many could not enter the temple, just as we could not enter paradise. The Magi could not remain with Jesus, nor could they return to do him homage, because Herod desired to kill Jesus. Those who violently took over the kingdom closed Paradise to us. When Jesus came and cleansed the Temple, he came as the king of peace to deal with those who had violently taken over the kingdom.

WHO TO WORSHIP

When Jesus entered Jerusalem, he was accepted as King and immediately went to the Temple. He drove out those selling sheep, oxen and doves, He turned over the tables of the moneychangers. He did what a king does, which is to save his people. By cleansing the temple he cast out the false gods. A sign that foreshadowed this was when Pharaoh's daughter accepted Moses into her household as Prince of Egypt. Moses entered this place where there were many false gods, just as Jesus did, in order to free the people from slavery to sin.

It is obvious that this was not the type of freedom the people of Jesus' time desired, because by the end of the week, he was rejected. From Palm Sunday to Good Friday, Jesus was accepted as King. Jesus had to make the decision to obey God his Father and to reject all offers from the devil. In his agony in the garden, he had three temptations similar to those after his 40 days of fasting. And, like Moses, Jesus chose the God of his people—the God of Abraham, Isaac, and Jacob.

Jesus revealed to his disciples that, *"The ruler of this world has been judged, condemned and cast out."* It is ironic that those who opposed Jesus had judged, condemned, and cast Jesus out from the people of God and from the world. He had his own exodus, just as Moses also had to leave Egypt. Of course, the main difference being that Moses left to avoid death, while Jesus accepted death, because this was the will of his Father. Jesus accepted a physical death in order to avoid a spiritual death.

Up to this point Jesus had never been separated from his mother. The similar pattern that Moses experienced, that of being conceived, nurtured and exposed at birth are even more prevalent in Jesus' life for this reason. This last time that we see that pattern when Israel accepted Jesus as King, he was still with his mother because she was an Israelite. When the Jewish people accepted Jesus as King, they had accepted his mother Mary as the Queen Mother.

HOW TO WORSHIP

Before he died on the cross, Jesus said to his mother, (18) *"Woman, behold your son."* Then he turned to the disciple whom he loved and said, *"Behold your mother." And from that hour the disciple took her into his home.* He took her into his home just as John the Baptist took Mary's voice into his home, which at the time was Elizabeth's womb. So Mary believed what she heard, and she conceived the word of God. But Andrew and John, the other disciple, asked Jesus, (9) *"Rabbi, where are you staying?"* and Jesus responded, *"come and you will see."*

So now Mary conceived what she beheld with her eyes, and John took her, whom he beheld with his eyes, into his home. But what is it that Mary conceived? What is it that she beholds with her eyes? She beholds the image of her son on the cross. What she conceived was the Bread from Heaven, the Word of God and the High Priest. She conceived everything that was in the Ark of the Covenant, because she is the new Ark of the Covenant, the one not made with human hands.

There was one last thing that she took in visually: the inscription written over Jesus' head (19) *"Jesus the Nazorean, the King of the Jews."* She is also the dwelling place for God's name. She at this point had conceived the image of her son before he died and entered the belly of the earth. So even in death, Jesus, in a mysterious way was not separated from his mother.

As in The Catechism of the Catholic Church section 635, (20) *"He has gone to search for Adam, our first father, as for a lost sheep. Greatly desiring to visit those who live in darkness and the shadow of death, he has gone to free from sorrow Adam in his bonds and Eve, captive with him."* St. John however, learned not only where Jesus was staying, but also how to worship as he witnessed the crucifixion.

WHERE TO WORSHIP

After 40 hours, God raised Jesus from the dead. Jesus resurrected on the third day, because God sent him back to free the new Israel, the Church, from slavery to sin. The resurrection is a symbol of a new birth, and the leaders among the Jews were willing to pay the soldiers to lie and say that Jesus disciples had stolen his body. Once again, at the moment of Jesus' birth they were trying to kill him.

Mary of Magdala, in contrast, wanted to hold onto Jesus. Because of the resurrection of Jesus Christ, those who witnessed that he resurrected on the third day realized that he was the Son of God. Pharaohs' magicians recognized after the third miracle that, *"This is the finger of God."* The seven plagues that God had inflicted the Egyptians revealed that He came to pass judgment on the gods of Egypt. Likewise seven demons were cast out of Mary of Magdala.

Mary of Magdala tried to hold onto Jesus, but from that time on the woman would not receive life apart from the man, as Eve attempted. She will receive life from God, when she is joined to the man. This symbolizes that the body will receive life when it is joined with the soul. I am not speaking of male and female in the literal sense, but of the woman as a reference to the body. She will receive life and be sustained in life by the acceptance of her place as man's helper. Order has been restored in the Kingdom of God. Jesus said to her, (21) *"Stop holding on to me, for I have not yet ascended to the Father. But go to my brothers and tell them, I am going to my Father and your Father, to my God and your God. Mary of Magdala went and announced to the disciples. "I have seen the LORD" and what he told her.* So this woman was changed. She was known as a sinner, but will be remembered as one who loved much. She represents every one of us sinners who collectively make up the church.

The church is a new creation, and it appears that Mary of Magdala brought the word of God to the disciples, but another way of looking at this is that after God formed the first woman he brought her to the man. In other words, the word of God brought Mary of Magdala to Peter and the apostles. It is a new creation made up of sinners, who will be remembered as those who love much.

Jesus dwelled on the earth for 40 days before he ascended to heaven. For 40 days, the apostles and all of Jesus' disciples are like the Israelites in the desert, because they have God as their King. When Jesus ascended to heaven, his disciples would see him no more, just as when Moses ascended the mountain and viewed the Promised Land before he died. Moses did not enter the Promised Land, but Joshua, Moses' aid from the very beginning, led the people into the Promised Land.

CHAPTER FOUR

When Christians Make Christ Present

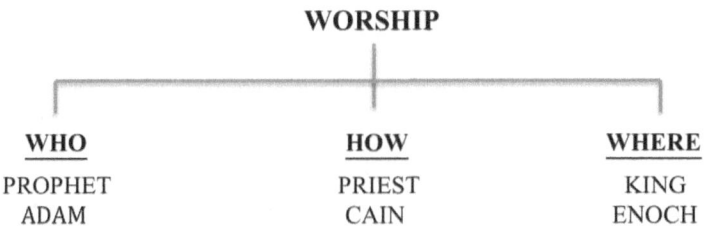

Jesus is the King of Kings. The church represented as the upper room is as the firmament that separates the waters in a new creation. Jesus sent his Holy Spirit at Pentecost to govern and guide his church in all truth. The Spirit of truth is the soul of the church, which makes us one body. This body of Christ was attacked immediately after Pentecost. Because Pentecost is the birth of the church, the infant was being attacked immediately because it was Christ who was being born out of the upper room.

First we see that Peter and John were put in prison and given a stern warning to stop teaching and preaching in Jesus name. Next Peter and the apostles were imprisoned, given a stern warning, and then flogged before they were released. It was during this time that St. Stephen was stoned to death. Afterwards Herod had St. James beheaded and St. Peter imprisoned, also with the intention of beheading him. Herod was not able to carry out his plans, because the angel of the LORD released St. Peter from prison. The early church members were experiencing the same rejection that Jesus Christ himself experienced, because it was Jesus who was being rejected and persecuted.

St. Peter was always included in the early persecutions because Christ gave the primacy of governing his church to the chair of Peter. Thus the Vicar of Christ, the Pope, suffers the same rejection that Adam, Moses, and all of the prophets suffered. Whenever the Pope accepts the office of the prophet, he obviously accepts the role of the suffering servant. When Jesus said, (22) *"the scribes and the Pharisees have taken their seat on the chair of Moses. Therefore do and observe all things whatsoever they tell you, but do not follow their example."* He demonstrates that the office must be respected, regardless of the person in that office. When we, the children of God, reject the prophet, we are easily drawn into the world.

The infant church had Mary Most Holy in its presence, and she was already experienced in these types of trials and tribulations. To their benefit, they were able to follow the example of their most Blessed Mother. The most holy Virgin Mary was Jesus' first disciple. We may call her the mother of all those who have faith, in the same way that we call Abraham the father of all those who have faith.

Those who have faith in God must also have trust. This can be difficult since God cannot be seen, but our Blessed Mother consented to God's plan of salvation even though she could have been put to death. Like Abraham, to say yes to God can mean death. When God told Abraham to sacrifice his son Isaac, this must have been difficult for Abraham to understand. The offspring he awaited all of his life, through which the promise seemed to have been fulfilled, would have been taken from him if he sacrificed the boy to God. So how could Abraham cooperate with such a plan, unless he had faith in God? When Isaac said to Abraham, (23) *"Father! Here are the fire and the wood, but where is the sheep for the holocaust? Son, Abraham answered, "God himself will provide the sheep for the holocaust."* The death of Isaac would mean that Abraham would not live on because he died without offspring.

It is also a similar circumstance with the Blessed Virgin Mary. When she consented to conceiving the Son of God, she was also willing to trust her life to God. The law permitted St. Joseph to put her to death, if she had committed adultery. St. Joseph was a righteous man and he was willing to obey the law. He was not going to listen to his wife and disobey God as Adam did. He would have obeyed God and not married her. He was also merciful, as he did not wish for revenge by having her put to death, but chose the option to put her away privately. This appears to be a sign of what God would accomplish in the incarnation. Finally mankind would receive the justice and mercy that the law could not provide. God revealed the truth to St. Joseph about Mary's pregnancy, and here again God provided the sheep for the holocaust.

Anyone who is favored by God in the way that our Blessed Mother is favored will be a target of envy. She was preserved from the original sin, and this makes her different from everyone else in creation, except Adam and Eve. This is another reason why her life was in jeopardy, but God preserved her by hiding the mystery.

We recognize her as the most exalted person in the church because of the great mystery of her relationship with the Trinity. We understand that the Father the Son and the Holy Spirit are a communion of love. Without love, there is no peace; without love there would be no sacrifice of the Son of God and therefore no communion. We are taught that Mary is the daughter of the Eternal Father, mother of the Eternal Son and spouse of the Holy Ghost Eternal. Anyone who prays the chaplet of the Immaculate Conception should be able to appreciate this mystery. It should deepen our love and devotion to our Blessed Mother, and our faith in God. The most holy Virgin also for this reason was never separated from Jesus, even in death. It is sin that separates us from God and from each other. Without sin there is no separation, only a communion of love. We are given something to strive for, to follow the example of our holy mother, the first and most perfect disciple of Christ.

Charles de Foucauld lived the hidden life of Jesus. As far as I know he did not explain what the hidden life of Jesus meant, but it is revealed in his life story. Like Mary Magdalene, he was known as a sinner, but is remembered as one who loved much. In this way, he has been an inspiration to many. When he lived for his own pleasures, he also had little respect for authority. At some point, he was converted and began a life that sought to please God. He lived not for himself anymore, but for Christ because Christ lived in him, as St. Paul explains it. He lived the mystery of the hidden life of Jesus. He made Jesus known in the way that our Blessed Mother exposed Jesus. It begins with the prayer of intercession for others, such as at the wedding feast at Cana.

Of course when Jesus is made known to the world there are consequences. The positive effect is the redeeming work of Jesus Christ. The negative consequences are whenever Jesus is exposed, his enemies are tormented. They will retaliate and try to do away with Jesus, but also with the one who made Jesus present. The demons asked Jesus, (24) *"What have you to do with us, Son of God? Have you come here to torment us before the appointed time?"* They can no longer hide in darkness, because Christ the light overcomes them. This battle will continue until the end of time, since there is no salvation for the evil spirits. Human beings have a similar struggle; especially when they hide from God for any reason. People may desire to remain in darkness, in order to preserve their life, and so will attack anyone they feels has infringed upon this freedom.

Christians should not be afraid to make Jesus present. If Moses were afraid, he would not have shown God's power before the Egyptians. He would not have been able to lead the Israelites out of slavery. If our Blessed Mother were afraid, she would not have given birth to our Savior. If Blessed Charles de Foucauld or any of the saints were afraid, they would not have made Jesus present at different times in history. It is our responsibility to have faith in God, and trust that he will preserve our life, even in the face of death. Jesus warned us that people love darkness because their deeds are evil. But we his disciples should want to make our good works known by bringing them into the light.

How are we to make Jesus present? First of all Jesus must be within us before we can make him present. This requires a life of prayer. It requires much prayer and a desire to be in full communion with the church. Yes, prayer puts us in communion with God, but sin separates us from God and the church. So we must learn what pleases God, and we must mature and become disciplined to avoid sin.

The realization that there is only one God gives strong compelling evidence that Christ is conquering the world. Yet there is still a great dilemma among believers who seek the one true living God. The question is how the one true living God speaks to us. From the time of the fall of humanity, we have been faced with this dilemma. Beginning with the first inquisition, (25) *"Did God really tell you not to eat from any of the trees in the garden?*

From that point on, the interpretation of the word of God determines whether humanity has peace or not. The true interpretation brings peace while error brings division. It is similar to when a couple marries and is in love with each other. They do not want to be apart, because they love each other and enjoy each other's presence. When the relationship becomes troubled, the peace they enjoyed is replaced with violence. It may not be a physical violence, but one that disturbs inner peace and emotions. This couple with high expectations will look for ways to resolve their conflicts, but there is something that cannot be agreed upon. They must desire to agree in the same way that humanity must desire the truth about who God is. If this cannot be agreed upon, the only resolution for the avoidance of conflict is to be apart. So the couple will separate from each other in order to avoid violence. It is the sad consequence of people who believe in love and would like to remain united but cannot agree on the perfect truth that would keep them together. The perfect truth is love and that love is self-sacrificing, as the only begotten Son of God has revealed to us.

There is much responsibility for those who are Catholic to preserve the unity of the faith. The mystery of the incarnation is present to us in many ways. A point of contention for many is how could divine revelation be made known to human beings. For this reason, many reject ecclesiastical authority. The Incarnation, the Resurrection, and the Consecration during the Holy Mass all reveal a person. It is the revelation of the divine person Jesus to human persons. So why is this difficult? It is difficult because in the same way our first mother Eve rejected the words given to Adam, we also reject established authority. Those who reject this human authority directed by God usually turn to angels, even if not intentionally. They believe that purity of their doctrine does not become corrupted through a mediator. This is the quickest and easiest way to be deceived.

We know whom it is that speaks to us from the invisible world by recognizing his voice in the visible world. It means that we know who is first in the invisible world by knowing who is first in the visible world. And for Catholics that person would be whoever sits on the chair of Peter. St. Peter is Prince of the apostles; the one to whom Jesus gave the keys to the kingdom. The Pope, the Vicar of Christ is first in our visible world. He is the voice just as John the Baptist and all of the Old Testament prophets were, giving an audible voice to the invisible word of God.

Anyone that God favors of course draws scrutiny from the world, and the envy of devils. We cannot take this lightly, lest we be drawn into the world. Although the world puts up much resistance and poses itself as an enemy to God, in a mysterious way the world wants to be conquered by God, because everything in creation belongs to God. In this way the world that opposes us because we belong to Christ, is also depending on us to remain faithful to the church.

The Christian who prays constantly and confesses his sins regularly is in a wonderful position to accomplish the will of God. All who receive God unto themselves are blessed, but also become blessings to others. Because God is so much greater than we are, he cannot be contained within us, and so he will burst forth as overflowing and we become as one giving birth to Christ. The natural response of the world is to put Christ to death immediately, but we should not be afraid. We follow in the footsteps of great heroes. Every one of the saints had to live this experience. They understood the importance of heroic virtue and knowledge of Christ. Many soldiers in God's military died for their faith. These are not casualties, but victories. We fight for the Kingdom of God because it is our duty. Anyone who loves God will fight in his army, the same way we fight for our country, which we love. Although we are obliged to fight by standing up for truth and revealing Christ and his love to the world, we have one great consolation. God has already declared victory. It is comforting to know that Christ has already conquered the world. Our concern is to know, love, and serve God in this world, in order to attain the happiness of heaven.

Endnotes

BOOK: Charles De Foucauld; Journey of the Spirit
Author: Cathy Wright Isj
- (1) Page 15 "Charles didn't feel…"
- (2) Page 7 "I love Our Lady…"

BOOK: The New Saint Joseph Baltimore Catechism No. 2
- (3) Page 9 "To gain the happiness…"

BOOK: NEW AMERICAN BIBLE
- (4) Genesis 2:16-17
- (5) Genesis 2:7
- (6) Luke 22:42
- (8) Luke 23:42-43
- (9) John 1:38-39
- (10) Genesis 3:10
- (11) Exodus 2:7-9
- (12) Exodus 4:24-26
- (13) Exodus 8:15
- (14) John 1:5
- (15) John 8:34-36
- (16) Genesis 4:13-14
- (17) John 2:3-5
- (18) John 19:26-27
- (19) John 19:19
- (21) John 20:17-18
- (22) Matthew 23:2-3
- (23) Genesis 22:7-8
- (24) Matthew 8:29
- (25) Genesis 3:1

BOOK: THE ROMAN MISSAL
- (7) Eucharistic Prayer I—93 "as once you were pleased…"

BOOK: CATECHISHM OF THE CATHOLIC CHURCH
- (20) 635 "He has gone to search…"

Acknowledgements

It was because of encouragement from family and friends that I endeavored to undertake this project. When sharing single line diagrams of Scripture insights, I was advised numerous times, "You should write this out." Finally, after I heard the same confirmation over the years, my spiritual director Father Bradshaw inspired me to start writing.

Thanks to everyone who heard God speaking to us and were so kind to offer encouragement. For my wife Jewell, the love of my life, for all the support needed and more, I thank God. To my daughter Rachel for help with English and grammar, and problem solving in general; I offer a big thanks. David my son, thank you for the PowerPoint presentations, help with Microsoft Word, and being my resource for all things concerning computers. Mrs. Katrena Parnell, for the edits and instructions at a time most needed, thank you and God bless. Thank you Mrs. Gladis Benavides, and Mr. Dorence Cooley for sharing your talents and resources, peace to you and your families. I would like to thank Dr. Mary C. McDonald for sound advice and encouragement. You are a great source of inspiration to many of us and we love you.

New book coming summer of 2014...

"Saul, Saul Why Do you Persecute Me?"

Imagine this: an allegory between Saul, the first king of Israel and Saul of Tarsus. Why did God stop speaking to King Saul? How is it Saul of Tarsus tried to destroy the Church, yet he became the great scribe known as St. Paul the Apostle? Explore these thoughts and more as we pilgrimage from slavery in Egypt to Pentecost, when God fulfilled the promise made to our ancestors. *Saul, Saul Why Do You Persecute Me?* is scheduled for release the summer of 2014. For more information on this book and future publications visit our website: www.deaconnormanalexander.com.

www.ingramcontent.com/pod-product-compliance
Lightning Source LLC
Chambersburg PA
CBHW031430290426
44110CB00011B/596